GW00630649

Office Design

Edited by/Herausgegeben von:
Fabio Fabbrizzi

 teNeues

For this edition:
© 2002 teNeues Verlag GmbH + Co KG, Kempen

For the original edition:
© 2002 Federico Motta Editore SpA, Milan

© of the authors for the photographs
Cover: Vallifuoco Pani & Steingut
        Sede di una società immobiliare
        Cagliari, Italia
        Photo: © Dessi & Monari, Cagliari

Original book title: Uffici

English translation: Nina Taranto
German translation: Margot Zander
Production: bookwise, Munich

Published in the US and Canada by teNeues Publishing Company
16 West 22nd Street, New York, N.Y. 10010, USA
Tel.: 001-212-627-9090, Fax: 001-212-627-9511

Published in Germany by teNeues Verlag GmbH + Co KG
Am Selder 37, 47906 Kempen, Germany
Tel.: +49-(0)2152-916-0, Fax: +49-(0)2152-916-111

Published in the UK and Ireland by teNeues Publishing UK Ltd.
Aldwych House, 71/91 Aldwych, London WC2B 4HN, UK
Tel.: +44-1892-837-171, Fax: +44-1892-837-272

www.teneues.com

While we strive for utmost precision in every detail, we cannot be held responsible for any
inaccuracies, neither for any subsequent loss or damage arising.

Die Deutsche Bibliothek – CIP-Einheitsaufnahme
Ein Titeldatensatz für diese Publikation ist bei der Deutschen Bibliothek erhältlich.

ISBN 3-8238-5578-6
Printed in Italy.

contents
inhalt

No longer keyed to mere functional requirements nor simply representing a productivity value, as Modern Architecture had imposed, office space is presented to the contemporary designer as a true architectural opportunity.

The origins of this portrayal go back a long way and to be able to understand it completely we need to go back to the idea of an architectural and functional typology that has undergone considerable and inevitable developments.

Office space, what we think of nowadays as the place where study and business activities take place, did not have its own functional perimeters and hence a recognizable architectural definition until the Renaissance. In fact, action and reflection were kept strictly separate, giving rise on the one hand to the idea of a place still linked to the commercial and banking function, and on the other hand to the idea of a place characterized by the search for privacy and intellectual contemplation.

The former was often found in the home, its space being distinguished not through a functional specialization, but simply through its separate use. This commingling featured in very distant geographical examples, such as the typical Renaissance palazzo of the Italian merchant cities and the North European business homes, but it was not strong enough to develop along a clear-cut evolution. On the other hand, the most isolated and reserved parts of the home were set aside for study.

The first building to combine the characteristics of both study and practice is the Uffizi gallery in Florence, by Giorgio Vasari, which also features a well-defined and innovative architectural character.

The Uffizi was based on the simplified layout of divisions into separate rooms, the so-called "audience rooms", connected to each other by a corridor.

The horseshoe design is the main feature of this building with regards to the city, but it remained the isolated archetype that another model of cellular organization was derived from.

The same idea of an area separated into closed rooms, connected by corridors, was established in the compact block building model that copied the palazzos, or later on, apartment buildings.

At the end of the 18th century, John Soane designed the Bank of England in London, offering an alternative model to the division into separate rooms. He created an interpretation of Roman architecture, creating a sequence of building sections, connected with each other through courts, arcades, vestibules and atriums. From then on, this became the other archetype in designing office spaces.

These two buildings, with their different innovations, unwittingly set the methods of design for office space, and ended up being the two different models that the entire evolution of this theme went through. For the entire 19th century there was still a kind of reciprocal contamination of the two models that was sensitive to the relationship the buildings ended up having on the urban level.

It was in the 20th century that the two visions clearly separated: in Europe, assigning to the corridor the true role of a volumetric organization principal, and in America, as a consequence of the skyward development of office blocks, the evolution of the office settled on an open space layout.

The best results came from a hybrid of these principals, architecturally overcoming this schematization to use them as a basis, incorporating them and developing them in a new direction. The Larking Building in Buffalo, New York, by Frank Lloyd Wright, built in the early 1900's is one example; the layout is based on an idea of open space but at the same time extremely controlled. A "machine" building, but respectful of nature, given this mark so as to take on a visible dimension of production but at the same time so aware of the needs of the people who worked there.

From those two current models, the one that became increasingly popular was the one connected to internal continuity, also because with the affirmation of the industrial culture we saw an interesting relationship between the invention of the space of the factory and that of the office.

This is why Modern Architecture ideally added the office area to the factory space, turning this place set aside for management, planning and supervising production into the brain of the factory itself. From this viewpoint, the open and fluid space became essential to carry out supervision, control and hence improvement of production.

The architectural qualities of these areas suffered; profound rationalization led to a general unifying of different spatial needs, reducing them to a limited series of common traits.

6 These traits partly copy those that are the points that all modern architecture is based on, in other words the open layout, the curtain-wall façade, the wall-to-wall windows, the theme of light.

These uniform characteristics inevitably led, on this and the other side of the ocean, to the open space taking over. A space marginally connoted and differentiated from the expressive point of view but strongly rationalized from the point of view of décor. Designers therefore turned their attention to furniture and accessories. This was the phase where a proto-ergonomic approach appeared, still seen however as a tendency to increase productivity and not as the exclusive well being of the user.

This supremacy of the productive aspects translated into the standardization and control of the intellectual dimension, giving rise to a characterization whose components appear to have an almost opposite mark. On the one hand, the tendency to create increasingly bigger and more open spaces and on the other hand, that of creating a process of standardization within these spaces that actually annulled this criteria into lots of the same repetitive and obsessive areas, which made the architecture simply mechanical.

In many cases, the internal flexibility became the main generator for creating the outside as well, adding anonymity to anonymity. If we then go on to add complete, totally mechanized control of the environment, we definitively annul any compositional reflection deriving from the features of the diverse positioning in different places.

In line with this loss of architectural identity, reactions to this state of matters developed, identifying completely innovative criteria and methods in conceiving the office area. The first reaction came from Germany at the end of the Sixties, where they developed a series of rules involving both the organizational apparatus and the spatial aspect. The spatiality favored more communication and exchange between office workers, annulling all the physical differences. The "office-landscape" aimed at improving general production by choosing communicative and functional aspects over bureaucratic and hierarchical restrictions. Architectural features became a neutral container where décor once again asserted its priority role. The other, which arose as an evolution of the "office-landscape", is the so-called "Action Office", a vision that emerged to overcome the conflict between the office worker's private and group dimension and offered a middle course between a concept of closed space and open space. It also provided the possibility of acting within a flexible layout of continuous equipment at the height of man, set out however so as to prevent complete closure.

The design of office space today is characterized by all these invariants, generating an extremely stimulating kind of compositional polyphony.

Never as in the last decade have we seen such a swift change in work methods following the increasingly rapid acquisition of information technologies. The office space has adapted itself to this revolution. It has slowly lost its sterile appearance that had distinguished it for so long; this was also because it had become inevitable for the office space to appropriate architectural typologies that emerged for other purposes because of the more and more frequent reuse and conversion of existing buildings, becoming the preferred place of mediation between design and architecture.

In fact, the space became a kind of office-territory that could be changed according to the different needs, or it was restricted to specific areas, supported by a new work mentality without set hours, rhythms and layouts; so new organisations were founded on complete flexibility, seeking well-being and increased creativity as well as optimal worker productivity.

Lastly the contemporary office tends more and more to take on a reassuring domestic image, ("office-home"?) using icons and symbols that are blended into its traditional imprints in a completely innovative manner, giving rise to a new and surprising design expressiveness.

Fabio Fabbrizzi

8

Die Gestaltung eines Büroraums stellt für den Architekten heute eine Gelegenheit zur Verwirklichung seiner Ideen dar, ohne dabei an rein funktionale und an die Produktivität mahnende Einschränkungen gebunden zu sein.

Diese Charakterisierung wurzelt im Konzept einer Typologie, die in architektonischer und funktionaler Hinsicht unvermeidbare, große Veränderungen erfahren hat.

Die moderne Auffassung des Büros als Ort, an dem zugleich studiert und gearbeitet wird, entbehrte bis zum Ende der Renaissance jeder erkennbaren architektonischen Kontur.

Zwischen der produktiven und der meditativen Tätigkeit verlief eine klare Trennungslinie. Erstere verfolgt kaufmännische Absichten und knüpft Beziehungen nach außen. Die meditative Tätigkeit richtet sich im Gegensatz dazu nach innen. In ihrem Mittelpunkt steht die Suche nach Intimität und intellektueller Betrachtung.

Der Ort für geschäftliche Belange befand sich sehr oft im Wohnhaus und unterschied sich von den anderen Räumen nicht durch funktionale Aspekte, sondern lediglich durch seine Zweckgebundenheit. Diese Art des Wohnens und Arbeitens unter einem Dach hat sich trotz bemerkenswerter geschichtlicher Beispiele wie die Renaissancepaläste Italiens oder die nordeuropäischen Handelshäuser architektonisch jedoch nicht weiterentwickelt. Zum Studium zog man sich in einen abgeschiedenen und intimen Bereich der Wohnstätte zurück.

Erst in den Florentiner Uffizien von Giorgio Vasari finden wir ein Architekturbeispiel, das die Merkmale beider, der meditativen als auch der schöpferischen Tätigkeiten miteinander vereint und sich darüber hinaus als funktional klar definierter und innovativer Gebäudetypus darstellt.

9

Die architektonische Unterteilung der Uffizien erfolgte in separate Räume, die so genannten Audienzzimmer, die über einen Korridor miteinander verbunden waren.

Der hufeisenförmige Aufbau des Gebäudes, das um einen Innenhof herum angeordnet ist, bestimmt nicht nur sein Verhältnis zur Stadt, sondern einen Archetypen, aus dem sich ein zellenförmiges Organisationsmodell entwickeln wird.

Dieser Gebäudeblock, wie man ihn vom Palasttypus oder später vom modernen Apartmentblock kennt, greift die Idee eines Raumes auf, der aus einzelnen Zimmern und Verbindungsgängen besteht.

Ende des 18. Jahrhunderts entwickelte John Soane mit der Bank of England eine Alternative zur Aufteilung in geschlossene Zimmer. Sein an die römische Architektur erinnerndes Bauwerk, das sich durch eine Abfolge von über Atrien, Laubengängen oder Höfen miteinander verbundenen Gebäuden auszeichnet, wird zu einem neuen Archetypen.

Diese beiden innovativen Gebäude bilden mit ihren unterschiedlichen Ansätzen die Grundlage, auf der die gesamte Entwicklung dieses Bereiches aufbaut. Noch im 19. Jahrhundert kann man eine gegenseitige Beeinflussung der beiden Stile beobachten, die stark auf ihr urbanes Umfeld Rücksicht nahm.

Erst zu Beginn des 20. Jahrhunderts erfahren die beiden Visionen eine klare Abgrenzung. In der europäischen Architektur wird der Korridor zu einem zentralen Element. In den Hochhäusern Amerikas setzt man hingegen auf eine Büroarchitektur der offenen Räume. Die Loslösung von diesen Schemata führt zu einer äußerst positiven Vermischung der Stile, welche die Entstehung von neuen Lösungen erst möglich macht. Das Anfang des letzten Jahrhunderts erbaute Larking Building in Buffalo, New York von Frank Lloyd Wright ist ein Beispiel für die Realisierung der Idee des offenen Raums, die mit einer sehr streng kontrollierten Gliederung einhergeht: ein Bürogebäude, das seiner Funktion und im gleichen Maße dem Menschen gerecht wird, der darin beschäftigt ist.

Die jetzige Strömung tendiert zum offenen Raum, was nicht zuletzt durch die industrielle Kultur erklärbar ist, die interessante Zusammenhänge zwischen Fabriken und Büroräumen aufzeigt.

Die Moderne sieht den idealen Raum für das Büro in der Fabrik, wobei dem Büro die zentrale Funktion der Planung und Überwachung der Produktion und als Folge daraus auch eine Steigerung der Produktion zukommt – ein Konzept, das nur im offenen Raum umgesetzt werden kann.

Für die Architektur bedeutet diese Strömung grobe Einschnitte in der gestalterischen Qualität, eine tiefgreifende Rationalisierung und eine weitgehende Vereinheitlichung der Räume.

Diese Merkmale decken sich zum Teil mit jenen, welche die moderne Architektur ausmachen, wie der offene Grundriss, die durchgehende Fassade oder das Spiel mit dem Licht.

Eine solche Vereinheitlichung der Stilelemente hat unweigerlich dazu beigetragen, dass sich der Typus des freien Raums sowohl in Europa als auch in Amerika durchsetzt. Räume, die sich nur marginal voneinander unterscheiden, lassen dem Architekten lediglich bei der Wahl der Einrichtung und der Accessoires ein wenig Spielraum. Und genau an diesem Punkt setzt der protoergonomische Ansatz an, jedoch nicht ausschließlich zum Wohle des Benutzers, sondern neuerlich zur Steigerung der Produktivität.

Der Faktor Produktivität verlangt die Standardisierung und Kontrolle der intellektuellen Dimension, was sich in einem krassen Widerspruch niederschlägt: Man tendiert zwar zur Schaffung von immer weitläufigeren und offeneren Räumen, die aber in ihrer Homogenität jeden Individualismus entbehren und sich mechanisch wiederholen.

Das äußere Erscheinungsbild einer Architektur hat sich zur Gänze der Flexibilität des Innenraums unterzuordnen. Die Folge davon ist eine banale Aneinanderreihung von anonymen Gebäuden, deren Komposition in keiner Art und Weise mehr ihr Umfeld widerspiegelt.

Angesichts dieses Verlustes der architektonischen Identität hat man begonnen, das Konzept des Büroraums neu zu überdenken und das Denken in festgefahrenen Schemata abzulegen und zu überwinden. Die ersten Versuche in diese Richtung wurden Ende der 1960-er Jahre in Deutschland unternommen, wo man eine Räumlichkeit entwickelte, in der Bürokratie und Hierarchie sowie alle physischen Zeichen der Differenzierung zugunsten des kommunikativen Austauschs in den Hintergrund treten. Dieser Ansatz wird mit dem Schlagwort „Bürolandschaft" bezeichnet. Der Raum ist neutral gehalten. Seine Gestaltung obliegt dem Individuum. Die Einrichtung wird zum zentralen Element.

Das so genannte „Action Office" ist eine Evolution der „Bürolandschaft". Dieser Ansatz zielt auf die Lösung des Konflikts zwischen der privaten und kollektiven Dimension ab und bietet einen Mittelweg zwischen dem geschlossenen und dem offenen Raum. Die flexible Anordnung der Einrichtungsgegenstände schafft gleichzeitig Privatsphäre und Gemeinschaft.

In unseren Tagen zeichnet sich der Büroraum durch eine äußerst stimulierende Vermischung all dieser Varianten aus.

Besonders in den letzten zehn Jahren hat die Arbeit infolge des rasanten technologischen Aufschwungs tief greifende Veränderungen erfahren, die auch den Arbeitsraum prägen.

Der Büroraum hat nach und nach sein aseptisches Aussehen abgelegt, das ihn über so lange Zeit geprägt hat. Räume und Gebäude, die bisher anderen Zwecken dienten, werden nun in Büroräume umgewandelt, in denen Architektur und Design eine Synthese bilden.

Es entsteht ein äußerst veränderbarer Bürotypus, der sich rasch jeder Anforderung seitens seiner Benutzer anpasst. Das Büro von heute greift auf eine völlig neue Art und Weise Ikonen und Symbole aus unserer häuslichen Welt auf, die uns eine vertraute Umgebung vermitteln („Büro-Heim"?). Diese Entwicklung geht einher mit einer neuen Gesinnung, die, losgelöst von fixen Arbeitszeiten und althergebrachten Methoden, auf eine Steigerung der Kreativität setzt. Ein Weg, der nur über das Wohl der Menschen zu erreichen ist, die im Büro arbeiten.

Fabio Fabbrizzi

Office Design

16

Oficina tecnica de Javier Alfaro
1997-1998

alfaro

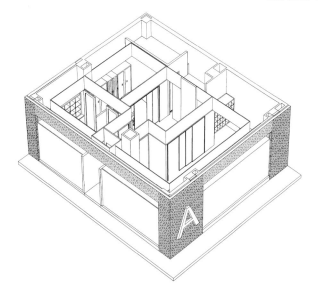

24

Ron Arad Associates Studios
1991

ron arad

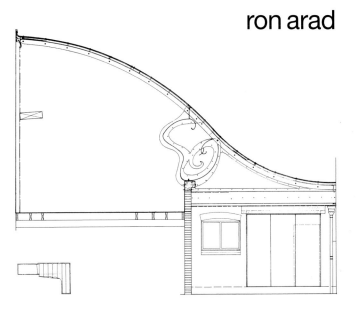

38

Office Architecture and Light
2000

architecture and light

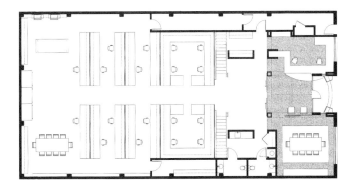

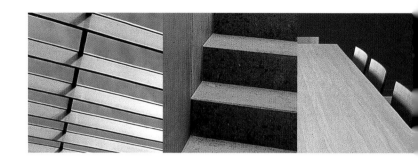

46

Van Hoecke nv
2000

bataille & ibens

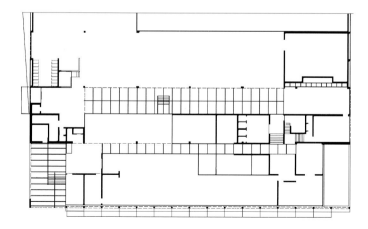

56

IDEO Product Development
1996

baum thornley

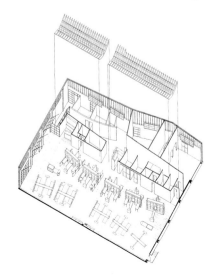

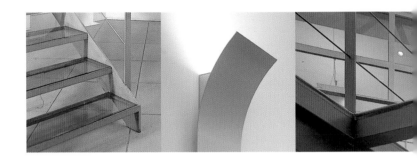

68

Studio Cassiopea
2000

boni conti giordano udom

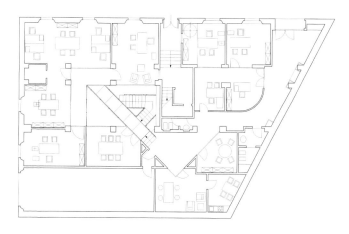

78

Uffici Paola Masini
1998-1999

boschi

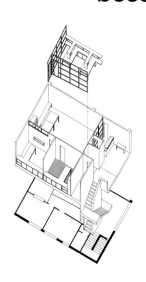

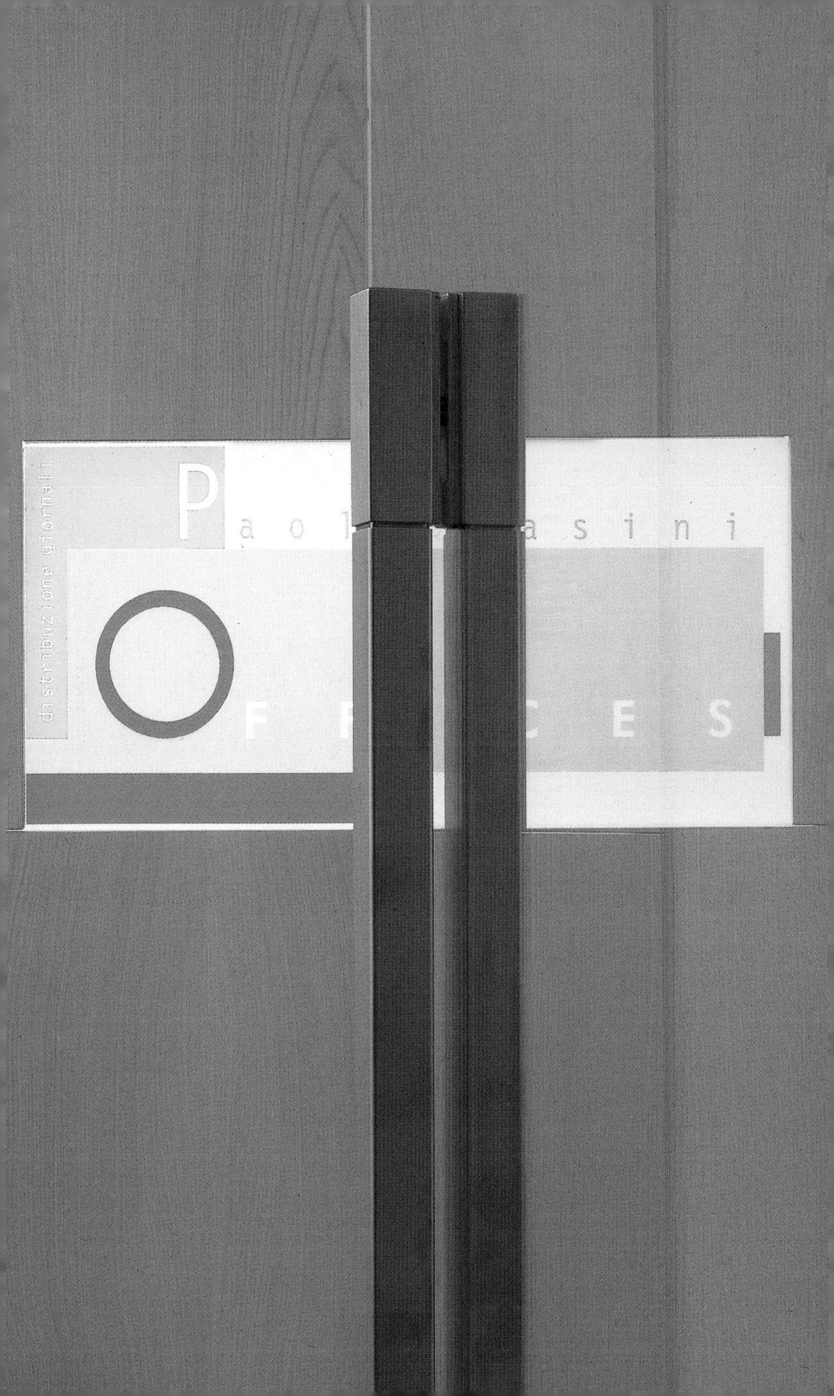
distribuzione giornali

Paul-Löbe-Haus,
Deutscher Bundestag
1997-2001

braunfels

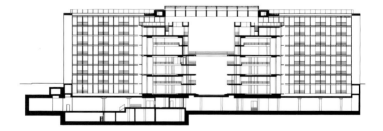

Studio professionale
1996-1997

calvi merlini moya

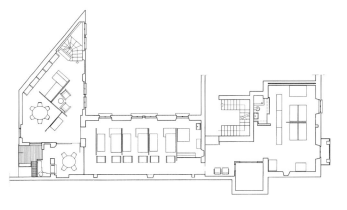

108

Bürohaus Mediaport
1997

chipperfield

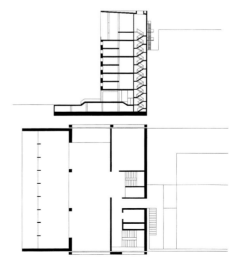

116

I. Net
2001

cibic & partners

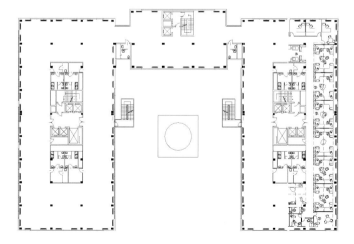

124

Raffin studio per commercialisti
1998

elastico

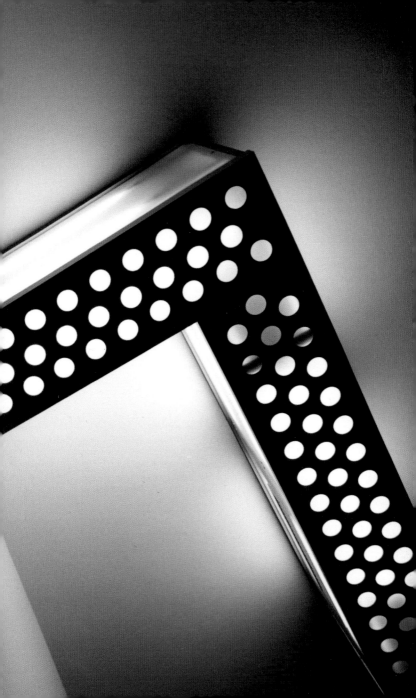

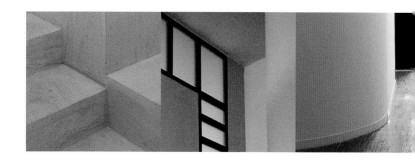

132

Editorial Centro Politécnico a Distancia
1990

esteban penelas

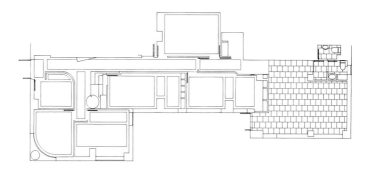

142

Edicions 62 Offices
1997

estudi idp

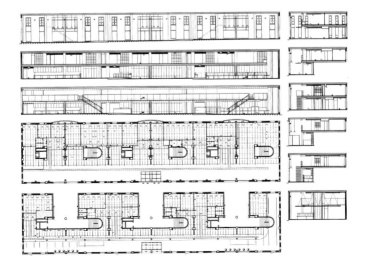

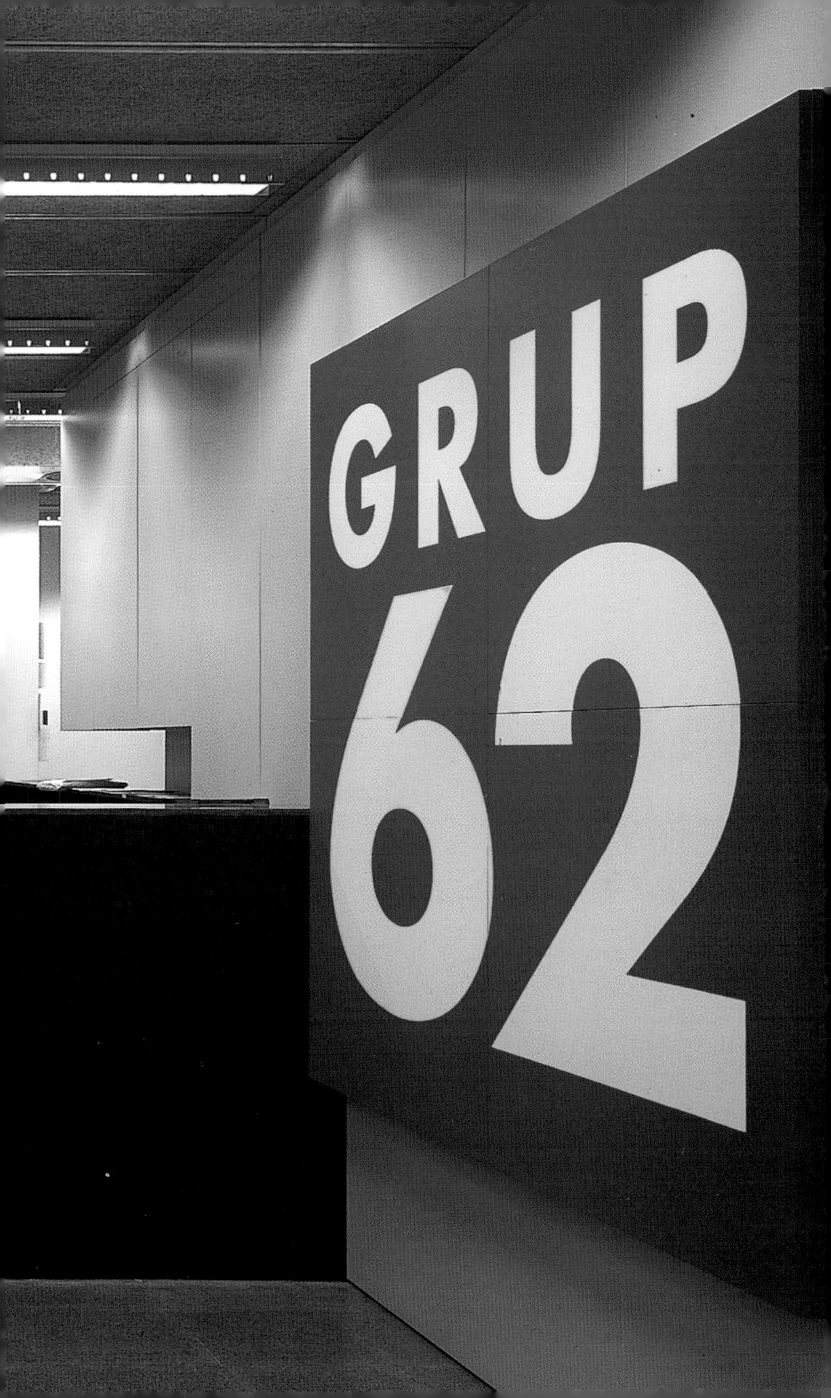
GRUP
62

P 62

ons 62
Empúries
Península
tral
re Català
uciones
lace
5 Editorial

154

"Mancinelli associati"
tax and business consultants
1993-1994

eusebi

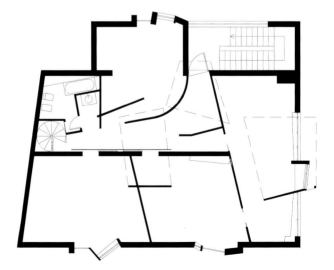

164

Headquarters
for the British Consulate-General
and the British Council
1992-1996

farrell & partners

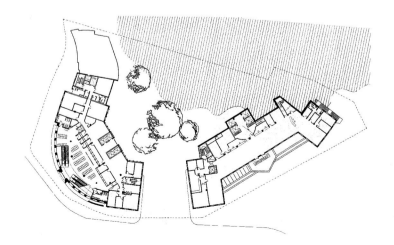

176

DHL Corporate Headquarters
1996-1999

gca arquitectos

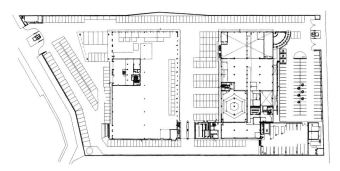

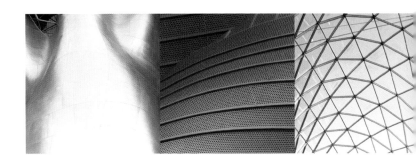

186

DG Bank
1995-2001

gehry

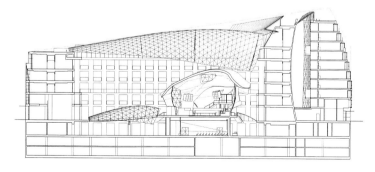

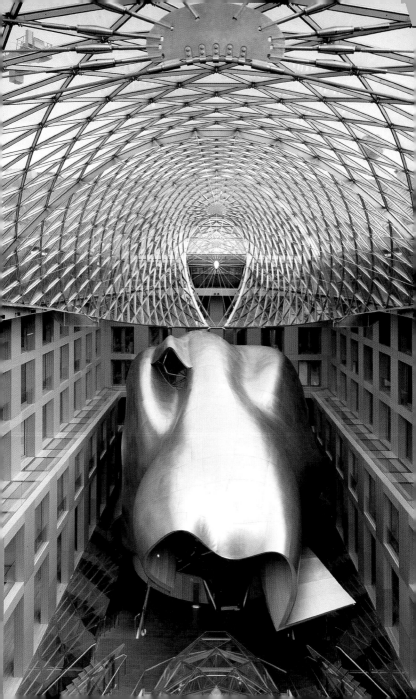

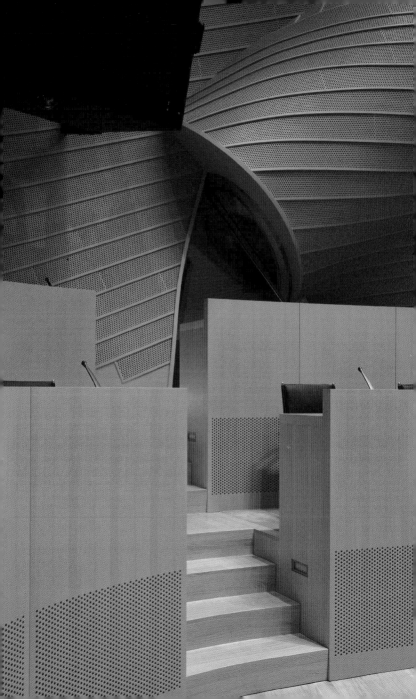

196

Hapag-Lloyd AG
1994-1995

gmp

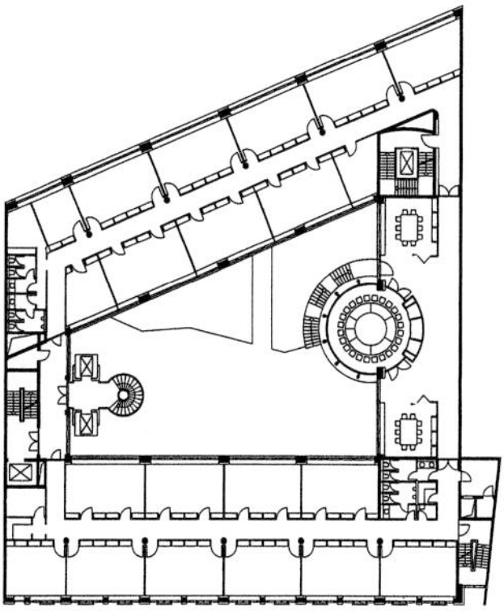

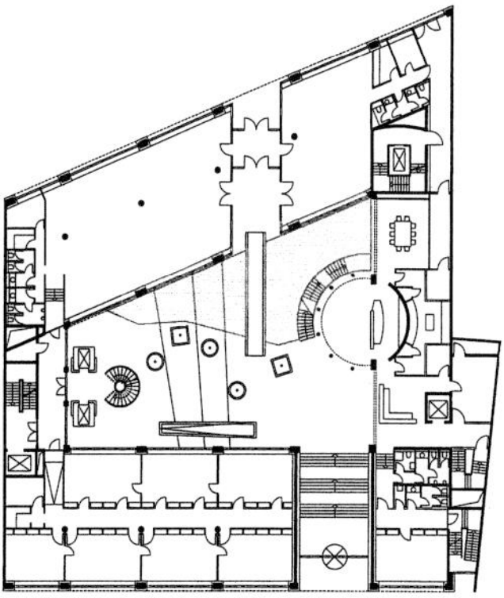

204

Werbeagentur Saupe Fouad
2001

kauffmann theilig & partner

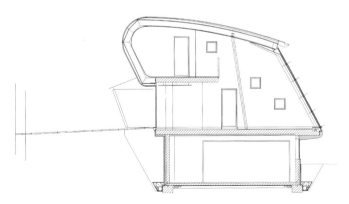

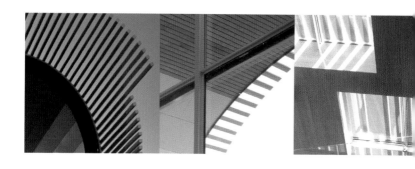

216

Verwaltungszentrum
Schuhhaus Werdich
2001

kauffmann theilig & partner

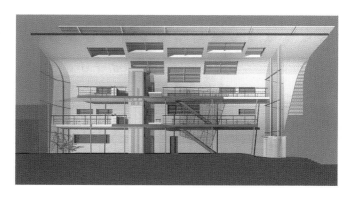

224

Tech Space
2000

kuwabara payne
mckenna blumberg

236

Ammirati Puris Lintas
1996-1997

kuwabara payne
mckenna blumberg

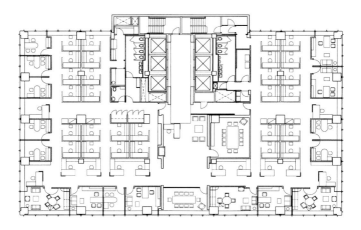

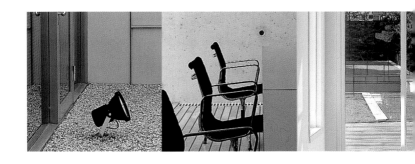

248

Maliebaan 16
1998-2000

mecanoo

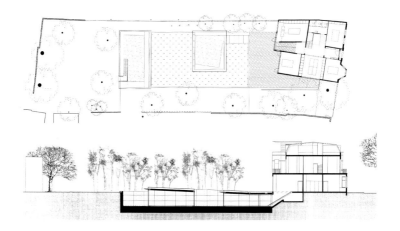

260

Lanza - Jean Klèbert
2001

micheli

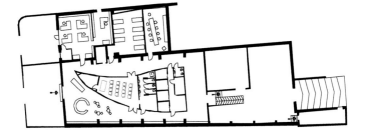

274

micheli

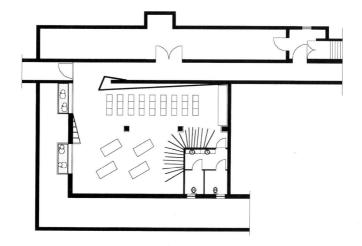

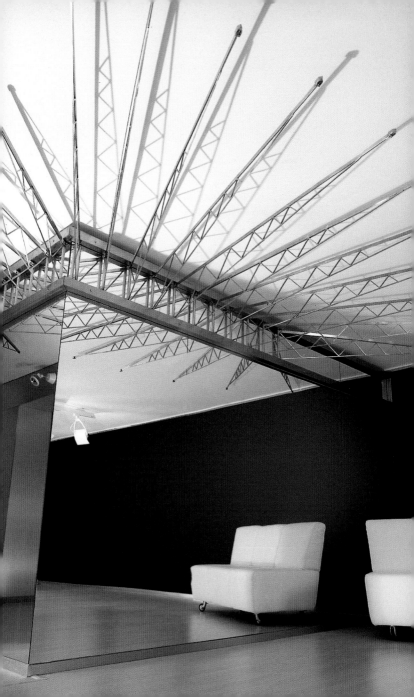

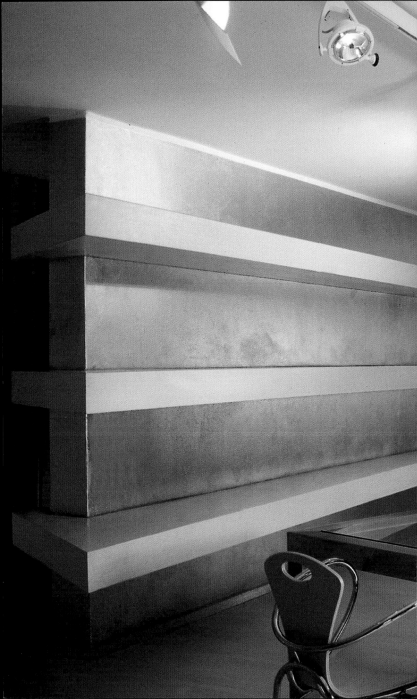

282

CLM/BBDO
1991-1992

nouvel

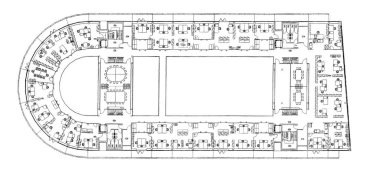

Siege Social Interunfall
1996-1999

nouvel

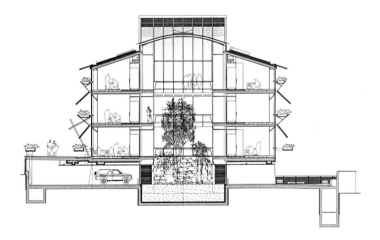

304

Renzo Piano Building Workshop
1989-1991

piano

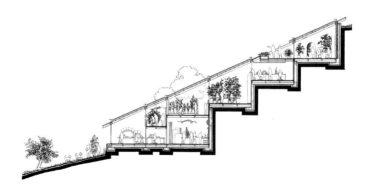

316

Uffici Eurogroup
1998

raffone & fiocco

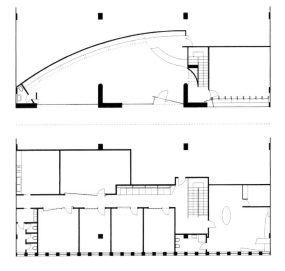

326

Unoaerre Italia s.p.a.
1999-2000

rba studio

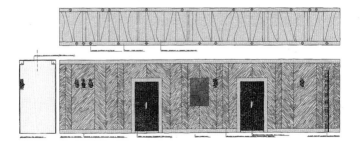

334

Oficinas Uniland
1998-1999

rumeu & gonzales

344

Caixa de Arquitectes
1991

sunyer & badia

354

D'Adda, Lorenzini, Vigorelli
Agenzia di pubblicità
1999

uda

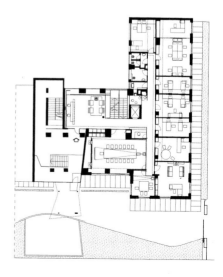

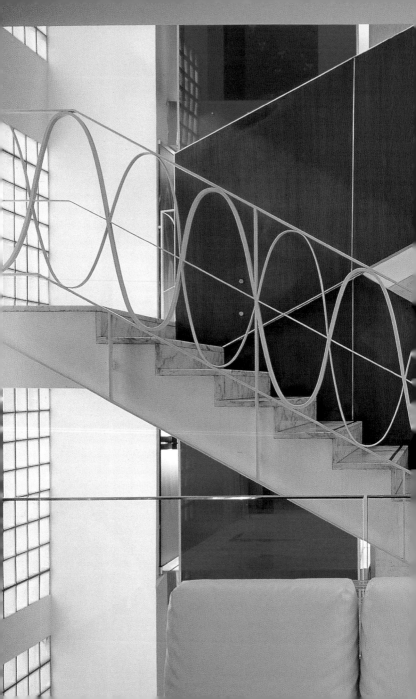

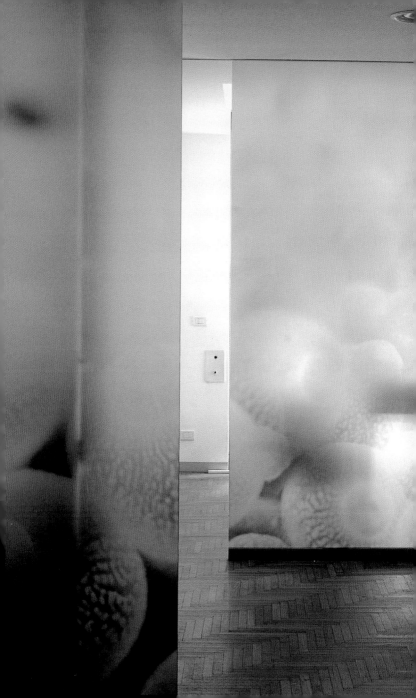

366

Sede di una società immobiliare
1996

vallifuoco pani & steingut

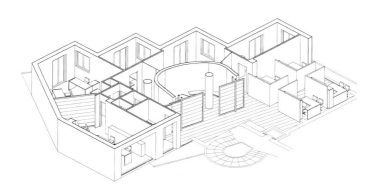

378

B. Braun Melsungen AG
1999-2001

wilford

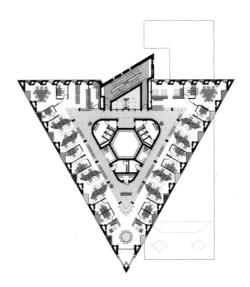

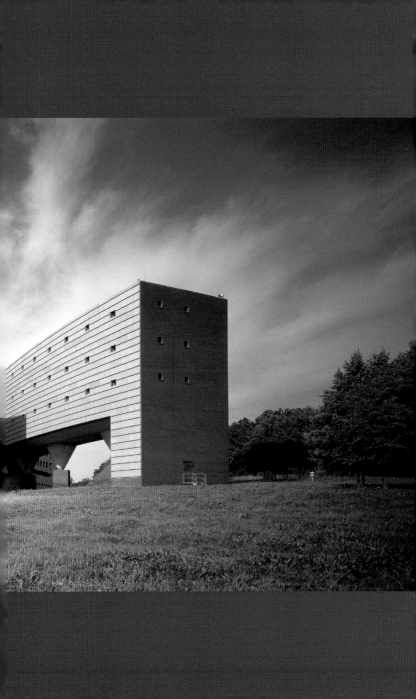